Amber's Atoms

The First 10 Elements of the Periodic Table

By E. M. Robinson   Illustrations by Susan McAliley

Design Friendly Press™

Seattle

Amber's here to greet you

And help you play the game

"This element — what is it?"

Can you guess its name?

Atomic Number 1

The world is made of atoms,

And these are very small;

The atoms of this element

Are the smallest of them all.

What is it?

Hydrogen Atom

Atomic Number 2

Most noble of the noble gases

This element's quite light;

Hang on tight to this balloon,

It could float up, out of sight.

What is it?

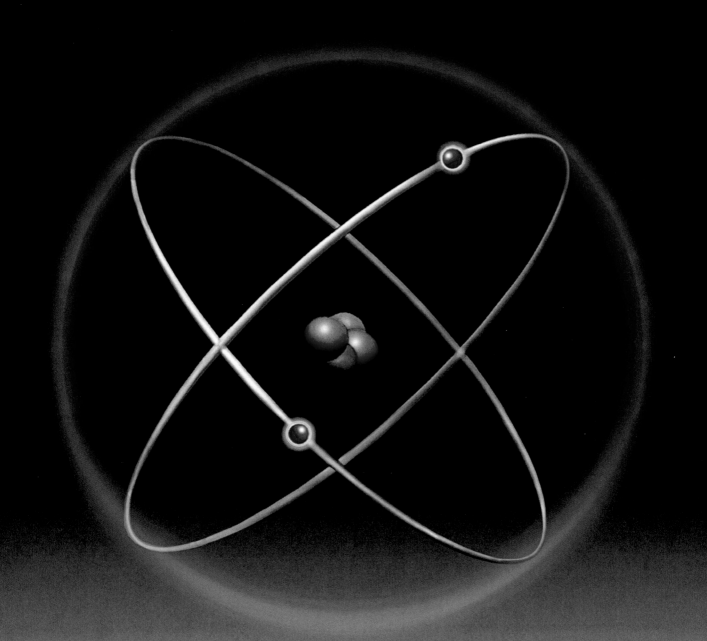

Helium Atom

Atomic Number 3

Known for its batteries,

Reusable and light,

This active little element

Makes compounds left and right.

What is it?

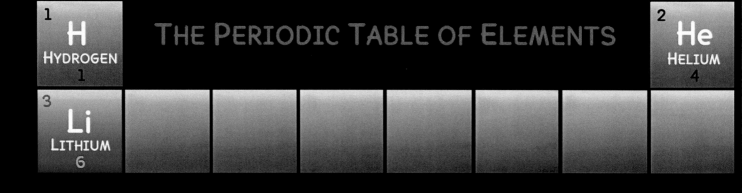

1 H HYDROGEN 1									2 He HELIUM 4
3 Li LITHIUM 6									

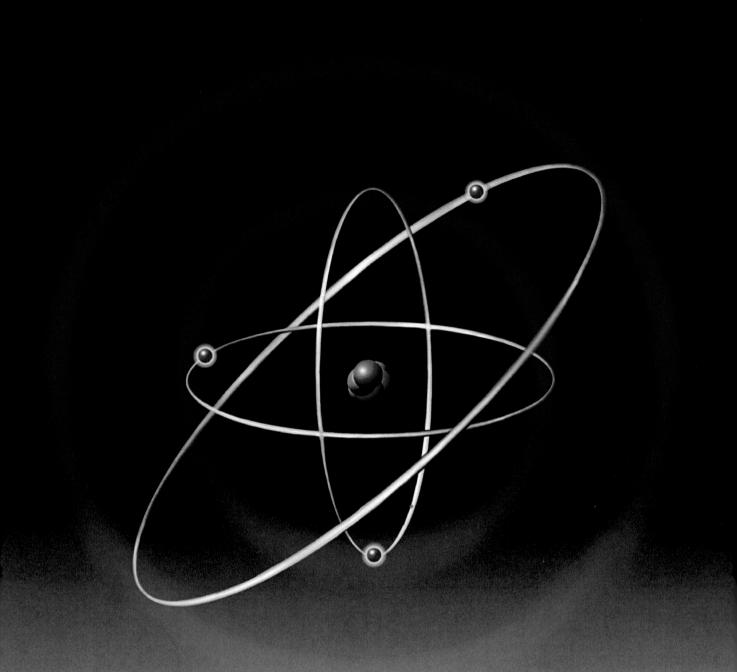

Lithium Atom

Atomic Number 4

Its name does rhyme with trillium

(The lovely woodland flower)

When combined with certain metals,

It can boost their strength and power.

What is it?

| 1 H HYDROGEN 1 | | | | | | | | 2 He HELIUM 4 |
| 3 Li LITHIUM 6 | 4 Be BERYLLIUM 9 | | | | | | | |

4

Be

BERYLLIUM

9

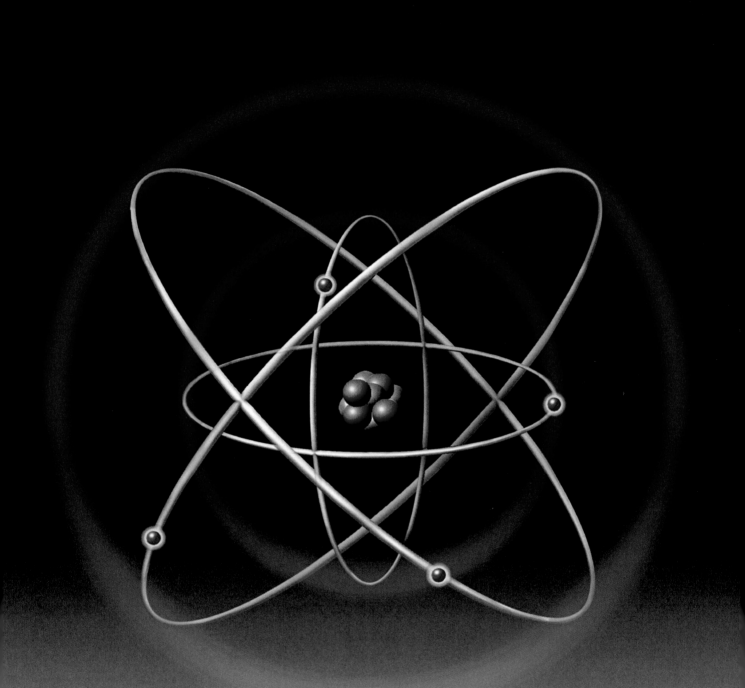

Beryllium Atom

Atomic Number 5

It gets its name from borax

And from carbon, it is true;

Its compounds clean and scour

And strengthen fibers, too.

What is it?

| 1 H HYDROGEN 1 | | | | | | | | 2 He HELIUM 4 |
| 3 Li LITHIUM 6 | 4 Be BERYLLIUM 9 | 5 B BORON 11 | | | | | | |

Boron Atom

Atomic Number 6

A most versatile of elements

You eat some every meal;

It's the base of Earthly life forms

And turns iron into steel.

What is it?

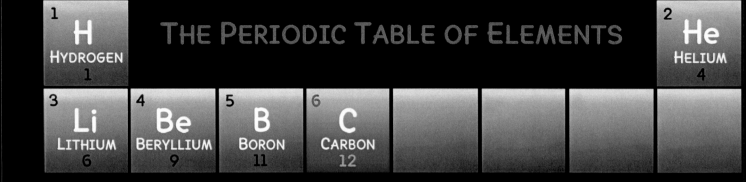

THE PERIODIC TABLE OF ELEMENTS

1 **H** HYDROGEN 1									**2** **He** HELIUM 4
3 **Li** LITHIUM 6	**4** **Be** BERYLLIUM 9	**5** **B** BORON 11	**6** **C** CARBON 12						

Carbon Atom

Atomic Number 7

This element while in the air,

Like a noble gas seems lazy;

But combined with C and H and O,

It could go BANG like crazy!

What is it?

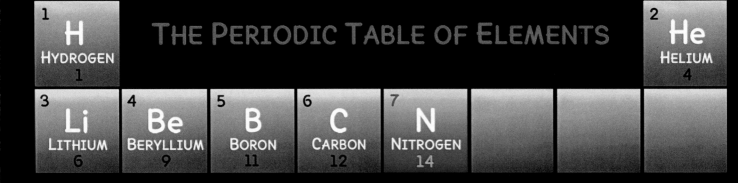

| 1 **H** HYDROGEN 1 | | | | | | 2 **He** HELIUM 4 |

| 3 **Li** LITHIUM 6 | 4 **Be** BERYLLIUM 9 | 5 **B** BORON 11 | 6 **C** CARBON 12 | 7 **N** NITROGEN 14 | | |

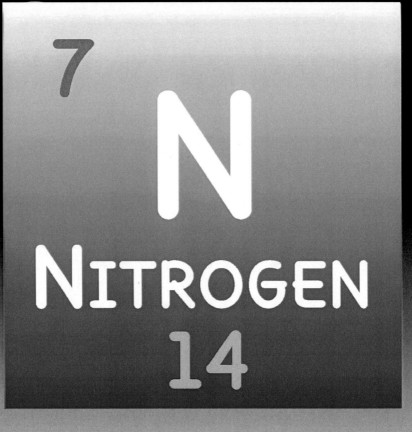

7

N

NITROGEN

14

Nitrogen Atom

Atomic Number 8

It oxidizes, bleaches,

And makes our iron rust;

It's in the sea for fish to breathe

And in the air for us.

What is it?

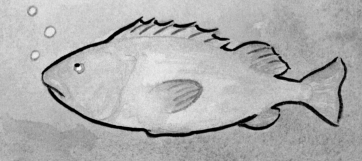

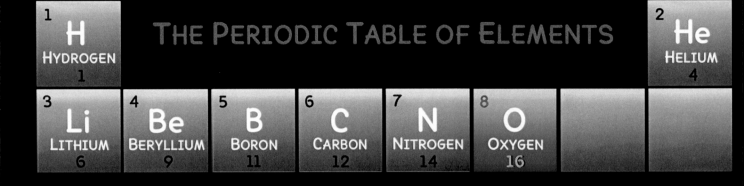

1 H HYDROGEN 1							2 He HELIUM 4
3 Li LITHIUM 6	4 Be BERYLLIUM 9	5 B BORON 11	6 C CARBON 12	7 N NITROGEN 14	8 O OXYGEN 16		

8

O

OXYGEN

16

Oxygen Atom

Atomic Number 9

Exceedingly reactive,

Extra greedy is this gas;

It's found in fluoride toothpaste,

And its acid etches glass.

What is it?

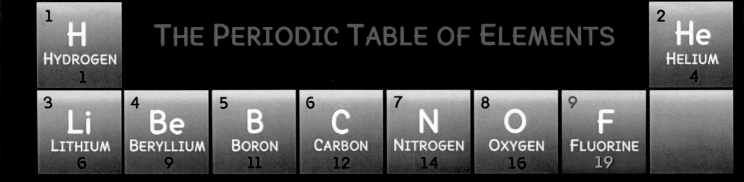

| 1 H HYDROGEN 1 | | | | | | | | 2 He HELIUM 4 |
| 3 Li LITHIUM 6 | 4 Be BERYLLIUM 9 | 5 B BORON 11 | 6 C CARBON 12 | 7 N NITROGEN 14 | 8 O OXYGEN 16 | 9 F FLUORINE 19 | | |

Fluorine Atom

Atomic Number 10

This gas is most famous

For brightly colored light;

It's inside flashy signs

That show up best at night.

What is it?

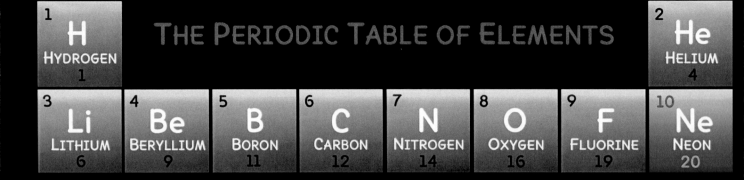

THE PERIODIC TABLE OF ELEMENTS

1 H HYDROGEN 1								2 He HELIUM 4
3 Li LITHIUM 6	4 Be BERYLLIUM 9	5 B BORON 11	6 C CARBON 12	7 N NITROGEN 14	8 O OXYGEN 16	9 F FLUORINE 19		10 Ne NEON 20

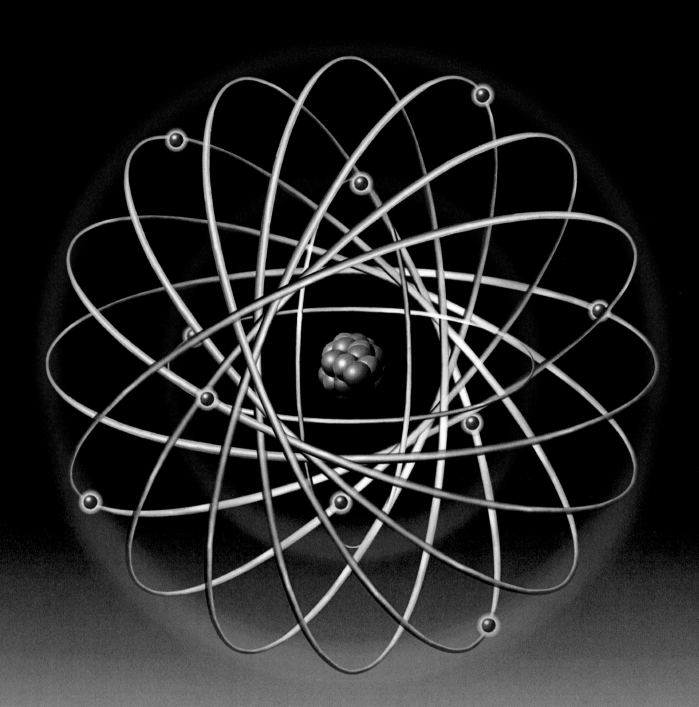

Neon Atom

Amber is all tuckered out,

She's curled up in her bed,

Fast asleep and dreaming,

With pillows for her head.

THE END

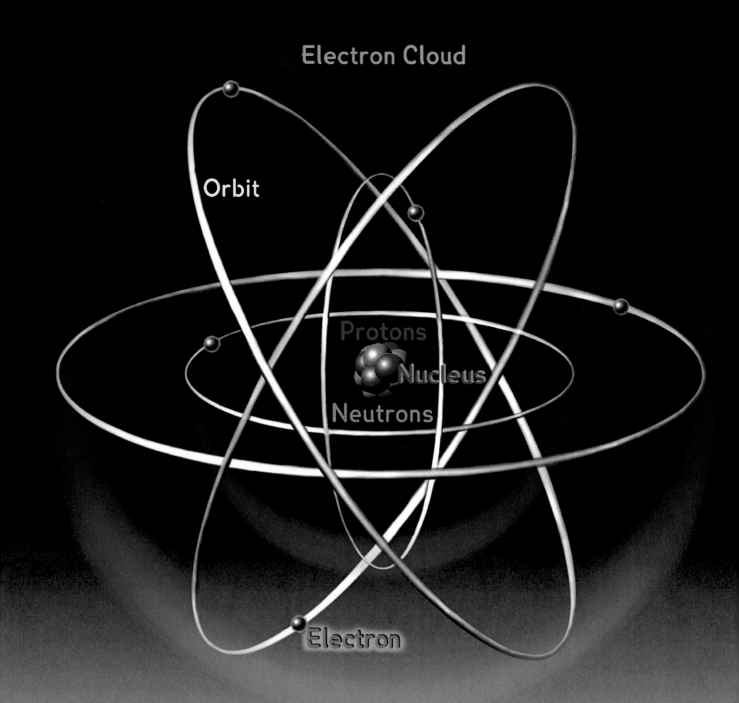

Electron Cloud

Orbit

Protons

Nucleus

Neutrons

Electron

Glossary

NOT DRAWN TO SCALE

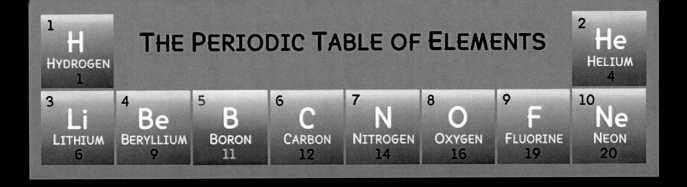

THE PERIODIC TABLE OF ELEMENTS

| 1 H HYDROGEN 1 | | | | | | | | | 2 He HELIUM 4 |
| 3 Li LITHIUM 6 | 4 Be BERYLLIUM 9 | 5 B BORON 11 | 6 C CARBON 12 | 7 N NITROGEN 14 | 8 O OXYGEN 16 | 9 F FLUORINE 19 | 10 Ne NEON 20 |

Count of Protons
"Atomic Number"

Symbol

Element

5

B

BORON

11

"Atomic Weight"
≈ Count of Neutrons + Protons

The Periodic Table of Elements

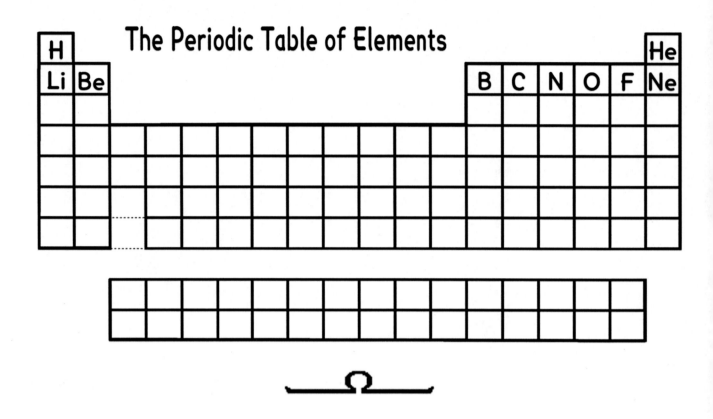

I would like to thank:

Susan McAliley - your art made the book;

My sister - your writing expertise and kind support made it better;

Larry Steele - your guidance kept the chemistry on track;

Donna Steele - your instincts kept the book appropriate for all readers;

Pat McFarland for your patience reading each revision through to the end;

Our golden Labradoodle Amber, who modeled with spirit and enthusiasm;

Kate Schoeffel of katesfamilypets.com for breeding the amazing Amber;

Joanna Penn and other generous writers for fostering Indie Authordom;

...and Dmitri Mendeleev – for organizing all those elements.

To VERONICA - Your love of learning sparked this book.

To JON - Your advice & wisdom made this book possible.

To BRITTA – Your generosity & caring made Veronica & Amber possible.

To CHRIS - Your love & support made it all possible.

With gratitude - EMR

To Matt – For your love & support of my creative lifestyle

To The Creator – For my life, Your love, & freedom of choice

To Liz - For inviting me into your dream creation

With gratitude – SM

Library of Congress Cataloging-in-Publication Data
Names: Robinson, Elizabeth Mary. | McAliley, Susan, illustrator.
Title: Amber's atoms the first 10 elements of the periodic table
/ by E. M. Robinson ; illustrated by Susan McAliley.
Description: Paperback edition. | Seattle : Design Friendly Press, 2016.
Summary: *A puppy illustrates a riddle describing each element,
followed by "What is it?", then its periodic table entry and atom.
Font and formatting chosen to help dyslexic readers.*
Identifiers: LCCN: 2015921077 (print) | ISBN 978-0-9970579-9-7
(softcover) | ISBN 978-0-9970579-8-0 (ebook)
BISAC: Juvenile Nonfiction / Science & Nature / Chemistry.
Subjects: Stories in rhyme | Children's picture book |
Chemical elements v Juvenile literature | Puppies | Dyslexia.
Classification: LCC PZ8.3 2016 (print) | LCC PZ8.3 (ebook)

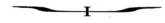

Susan McAliley created the full-color illustrations
with watercolor and gouache on 100% rag, archival watercolor paper.
E. M. Robinson created the tables and atoms in Adobe Photoshop®.

Made in the USA
San Bernardino, CA
20 October 2016